YOUR KNOWLEDGE HAS VALUE

- We will publish your bachelor's and
  master's thesis, essays and papers

- Your own eBook and book -
  sold worldwide in all relevant shops

- Earn money with each sale

Upload your text at www.GRIN.com
and publish for free

Bibliographic information published by the German National Library:

The German National Library lists this publication in the National Bibliography; detailed bibliographic data are available on the Internet at http://dnb.dnb.de .

Imprint:

Copyright © 2007 GRIN Verlag, Open Publishing GmbH
Print and binding: Books on Demand GmbH, Norderstedt Germany
ISBN: 9783656482482

This book at GRIN:

http://www.grin.com/en/e-book/153936/e-journalism-how-does-electronic-journalism-differ-from-traditional-journalism

Sebastian Plappert

E-Journalism - How does electronic journalism differ from traditional journalism?

GRIN Publishing

ICOM 817 Transnational Communication

Sebastian Plappert

How does electronic journalism differ from traditional journalism?
Going online - news communication in transition.

Globalisation describes the integrational process of growing interdependence and the worldwide flow of ideas, goods, capital and people across national borders (Meyer 2007, p. 262). From an economic point of view globalisation refers to the emergence of one single world market transcending national boundaries; international production and transactions render territorial location meaningless (Scholte 2006, p. 602-608). Due to the advent of new communication technology, in particular the internet since the 1990s, information and news are accessible online 24 hours a day and all around the globe (Aronson 2006, pp. 622-625). Accordingly, this essay will argue that this new form of news delivery influences traditional journalism and changes the mode of communication with audiences. After a brief examination of journalism, the paper will take a closer look at online news and globalisation, before turning to the current development of online news.

Conceptualising journalism

Journalism is a form of communication to transmit information to the public (Carey 1989). This could happen through elite experts interpreting the news (Lippman 1922), or as a process of interaction between journalists, citizens and experts in particular fields (Dewey 1927). Both conceptions eventually conclude that "the primary purpose of journalism is to provide citizens with the information they need to be free and self-governing" (Kovach & Rosenstiel. 2001, p. 17). Thereby, journalistic work is to report "stories that tell accurately and impartially about reality that exists independently from these stories and outside of the journalistic institutions" (Dahlgren 2001, p. 78). Accordingly Dasselaar (2006, p. 46) states that "journalism is truth seeking storytelling aimed at citizens, which is editorially independent". The generation of a 'public sphere' enables citizens who have no individual influence on governing powers, to discuss public affairs (Habermas 1989). Even though the role of the media "in providing information, analysis, forums for debate and a shared civic culture is beyond dispute" (Dahlgren 2001, pp. 64-65), journalism is also something else.
Despite this definitions describing journalism as the 'watchdog' of democracy, the primary purpose of the free press as a business is to make profit (Scott 2005, p. 90). Therefore, the choice of news-worthy stories made by traditional media is driven by potential interests of the

audience. The more copies of a printed newspaper are sold, the more profit is made; not primarily because of the direct sales, but because of advertising revenues (Scott 2005, p. 94). Since the costs of establishing news networks and producing media are enormous, "news has traditionally functioned as a natural monopoly" for big corporations (Scott 2005, p. 94). Moreover, most news outlets operate on a local level in order to define its audience for their advertising clients. Even national TV shows or newspapers are bound to a certain region defined by language or area of coverage.

News going online

Since the global spread of new media and the possibility to connect to the world via the internet, the character of the 'news landscape' is in transition. New technology has enabled information to be published instantly. Online news sites have the ability to update its content as often as the size of the staff allows (Thurman 2007). Consequently, there is no reason for customers to wait for the newspaper to be printed, all news are accessible in the internet before paper copies are available. Since the introduction of the internet has sped up the news process, journalist spend more time in front of their computer instead of investigating stories in personal and the verification of stories is far more difficult than before (Garrison 2000). Additionally, "publishing the news on the web costs roughly half of delivering print copy" and far less personnel is necessary to maintain an online news site than to publish paper news (Harper 1998, p. 70). On the other hand, these "low production costs have inspired millions to self-publish and millions more to read alternative content outside the mainstream" (Scott 2005, p. 92). Even though fewer customers buy print copies, they do not automatically resort to the online version of the same newspaper, but to various news outlets.

Consequently, money that "could be saved in production and distribution expenses [is] lost in the total lack of sales" (Scott 2005, p. 97). Given the variety of sources, nobody is willing to pay for general news delivered online and profit has to be made through advertising (Scott 2005, p. 100). Regarding the growing amount of websites and news portals, online advertising prices are low; there is just more 'supply' than 'demand' (Small 2000, p. 42). Furthermore, the average time spend on a news page is less than 30 seconds a day (Piller 2000), resulting in even fewer clicks on advertised banners or links (Finberg & Stone 2001, p. 43). Unlike in print, advertisers pay only "according to the number of times their advertisement is seen or clicked on rather than simply for space on the page" (Thurman 2007, p. 299). In order to attract advertisers, websites have to deliver target audiences and new ways of attracting readers online have to be found (Scott 2005, p. 97). One way to boost visits is to exploit the full range of technological possibilities of the virtual world.

Websites offer the possibility to hyperlink to other websites and confirm content or present dissenting arguments. However, this option could be used to refer to external sites as well as to link various pages within the same domain and deliver one-sided information (Deuze 2003, p. 212). Moreover, the internet can provide information in different formats to attract as many people as possible. This could enhance and improve the process of communicating news, but if "multimedia is used with no thought as to the reasons why it is being used, or it has poor lay-out or content it can result in a pointless aesthetic fiasco that needlessly hogs bandwidth" (Guay 1995, p. 5). Additionally, the internet offers the option to address audiences as active participants instead of passive consumers (Pavlik 2001, p. 125). Interactivity in form of navigatable content, discussion forum or the adjustment of personal preferences allows users to take part in the process of generating news (Massey & Levy 1999, p. 526). By adapting to new technologies, journalists' way of working is changing.

Globalisation of online news

Furthermore, being a global medium, the internet renders national or regional boundaries meaningless (Seib 2001, p. 100). "The web offers unique opportunities to create a new form of interactive communication within the global community" with no regard to physical distances (McKinley 2001, p. 155). Consequently, "news readers could now read the *London Times* just as easily as the *New York Times* or catch the headlines from BBC instead of CNN", no matter from where they access the web (Scott 2005, p. 95). "The web offers a relatively level playing field for online news publishers", with the parent print brand being not an important factor on the international market (Thurman 2007, p. 302). Since distribution costs are irrelevant, global access is possible (Boczkowski 2004, p. 64). Especially online news outlets operating in English attract a growing numbers of readers which are not located in the same country than the newspaper (Thurman 2007, p. 287). Most of these international readers are forwarded from portals or search engines, responding to queries or because of one particular story (Thurman 2007, p. 291). "If a story is fresh and had caused considerable original reporting to be generated it is considered important" and appears on the Google news site (Bharat 2003, p. 9). However, Google refers to the earliest appearance and thereby favours fast news outlets without regard to quality or in depth reporting.

Since news publishers have to react as fast as possible and still be cost-effective, "the vast majority of news available on the web comes from the news wire services" like Reuters or AP

(Maynard 2000, p. 49). Whereas "e-journalists seek to maximise their readers through narrowcasting to assumed interests of commercially constituted groups" (Wilson & Tan 2005, p. 404), the choice of stories is limited. However, these online wire services allow online news outlets to select stories according to their target audience and set up specified 'international news' pages. Thereby, news websites avoid audiences being "confronted by complicated 'distant' references" and prevent "the audiences' consequent loss of interest" (Wilson & Tan 2005, p. 406). Since readers are attracted by familiarity and stories they can relate to (Wilson & Tan 2005), global journalism is always local at the same time. The hypertextuality of online news pages allows users to escape the linear narrative of traditional news and click themselves through only those parts that matters to them (Wilson 2004). International audiences perceive the same news differently, but their individual choice defines which information they gather. Consequently, they are not consistent readers of a particular online newspaper, but coincidentally attracted internet users to single stories.

Implications for electronic journalism

Mainstream news sites like those of CNN, BBC or MSNBC present news similar to printed newspapers (Jankowski & Van Selm 2000). Online content is considered 'shovel-ware', because "journalistic efforts online are still primarily intended as 'advertisements' for their parent medium, with hardly any interactive, multimedia and/or hypertextuality features" (Deuze 2002, p. 87). Thereby, "online journalism is […] a supplement and a complement to the dominant print and broadcast news media" (Scott 2005, p. 93). The internet works primarily as a distributional tool for traditional news, it presents the same content than printed newspapers online (Kramer 2002); stories "differ very little online from those printed in the originating newspapers" (Barnhurst 2002, p. 477). In order to attract broader audiences, both international and national, online news media has to follow a different kind of media logic; one that "points to specific forms and processes, which organize the work done within a particular medium", in this case the internet (Dahlgren, 1996, p. 63).

However, the common approach, aimed at cost-effectiveness, is to 'converge' the news production of different media types. 'Convergence' describes the centralized promotion of stories across different media and the streamlining of its distribution in multiple formats (Breckenridge 2000). This cooperation of media companies is achieved because "news outlets are forming content sharing partnerships at a dizzying clip, each trading on its own strength" (Shepard 2000, p. 24). As a consequence, "diversity may be decreased, as fewer reporters for any one media company may cover individual stories", but production costs are minimised as well (Pavlik 2001, p. 104). "Under this dispensation, the representative figure in journalism is no longer the citizen but the consumer, not the reporter or even the publisher but the shareholder" (Carey 1999, p. 50).

Thereby, "the paradox is that news organizations use expanding technology to chase not more stories but fewer" (Kovach & Rosenstiel 2001, p. 141). A growing number of individuals prefer to get their news from various different sources apart from media corporations, whose interests define what makes the news (Kovach & Rosenstiel 2001, p. 137). Since "the media oligopoly held in place by expensive production and geographic markets did not fly online", the internet leaves room for alternative perspectives of news (Scott 2005, p. 97). Whereas the quality of mainstream journalism online is in decline in general, alternative ways of communication provide possibilities to balance this development.

Journalism and blogging

One option to "reengage an increasingly distrusting and alienated audience" is possible participation (Pavlik 2001, p. xi). Whereas mainstream news publishers just release information, with little indication of sources and even less possibilities to oppose, the internet has given birth to new forms of news communication. Individuals publish weblogs, an online diary, which "is a form of writing that is unique to the web, reliant on what is arguably its key characteristic: the hyperlink", are just one example (Matheson 2004, p. 445). In contrast to mainstream sites, where opinion polls or discussion boards are "a supervised playground for users where their contributions never impinge on or shape the news", blogs allow real two-way interaction (Quinn & Trench 2002, p. 33). Following Blood (2000) blogs provide not only stories by linking to other sites, but also various personal opinions from different perspectives. A blogs works as an index of hyperlinks to a particular topic. Thereby, the "line between journalism and other forms is blurred by the many news-related weblogs maintained by people who are not employed as journalists" (Matheson 2004, p 449). Topics that do not come up in a traditional newsroom can be addressed and followed more deeply, because there is no financial pressure (Lascia 2002). Weblogs refer to mainstream new sites as well as to other sources; they offer different views on certain topics or at least an obviously biased perspective. Thereby they use all technical possibilities the internet offers to please potential audiences, which are an active part in blogging.

A new form of journalism

In conclusion, the internet offers the possibilities to change the one directed communication process into an interactive one. Mainstream media outlets are still very much bound by traditional forms of communication, but alternative sources force commercial newsrooms to react. In an age of globalisation, audiences have the ability to choose their source of information online and to be a part in the process of generating news. The distinction between audience and journalist has dissolved; both are at the receiving end as well as at the transmitting end of information. Since this process is still in its beginning, online journalism and news communication provides a rich field of future research.

REFERENCES:

Aronson, J. D. (2006). "The Communication and Internet Revolution". In Baylis, J. & Smith, S. (eds.), *The Globalization of World Politics*, 3rd edn., Oxford: Oxford University Press, pp. 621-643.

Barnhurst, K. (2002). "News Geography and Monopoly: The Form of Reports on US Newspaper Internet Sites". *Journalism Studies,* 3(4), pp. 477-489.

Bharat, K. (2003) "Patterns on the Web". In Nascimento, M., de Moura, E. & Oliveira, A. (eds) *Lecture Notes in Computer Science 2857*, Berlin: Springer, pp. 1-15.

Boczkowski, P. (2004). *Digitizing the News: Innovation in Online Newspapers*. Cambridge: MIT Press.

Carey, J. W. (1989). "A cultural approach to communication". In: *Communication as Culture*. New York: Routledge, pp. 13-36.

Carey, J. W. (1999). "In Defense of Public Journalism". In Glasser, T. (ed.), *The Idea of Public Journalism*, New York: Guildford, pp. 49-66.

Dahlgren, P. (1996). "Media Logic in Cyberspace: Repositioning Journalism and Its Publics". *Javnost/The Public* 3(1), pp. 59-72.

Dahlgren, P. (2001). "The transformation of democracy". In Axford, B. and R. Huggins, *The new media and politics*. London: Sage, pp. 64-88.

Dasselaar, A. (2006). The fifth estate. On the journalistic aspects of the Dutch blogosphere. MA Thesis. Leiden University.

Deuze, M. (2001). "Understanding the impact of the Internet: On new media professionalism, mindsets and buzzwords". *Ejournalist* [online], 1(1). Retrieved 18. October 2007. http://www.ejournalism.au.com/ ejournalist/deuze.pdf

Deuze, M. (2003). "The web and ist journalisms: considering the consequences of different types of newsmedia online". *New Media & Society*, 5(2), pp. 203-230.

Deuze, M. & Dimoudi, C.(2002) "Online journalists in the Netherlands: Towards a profile of a new profession". *Journalism* 3(1), pp. 85-100.

Dewey, J. (1927). *The Public and Its Problems*. New York : Henry Holt & Co.

Finberg, H. & Stone M. L. (2001). "Digital Journalism Credibility Study". *Online News Association* [online]. Retrieved: 13. October 2007.
http://www.journalists.org/Programs/ona_credibilitystudy2001report.pdf.

Garrison, B. (2000). "Diffusion of a New Technology: On-line Research in Newspaper Newsrooms". *Convergence* 6(1), pp. 84-105.

Guay, T. (1995). "Web Publishing Paradigms". *Information Technology Project Group paper* [online]. Retrieved 18. November 2006,
http://www.smcc.qld.edu.au/infotech/Paradigm/

Habermas, J. (1989). *The structural transformation of the public sphere*. Cambridge, MA: MIT Press.

Harper, C. (1998). *And That's theWay ItWill Be*. NewYork: NewYork University Press.

Jankowski, N.W. & Van Selm, M. (2000). "Traditional Newsmedia Online: an Examination of Added Values". *Communications* 25(1), pp. 85-101.

Kovach, B. & Rosenstiel, T. (2001). *The elements of journalism: What newspeople should know and the public should expect*. New York: Crown.

Kramer, S. D. (2002). "What's Changed? Everything and Nothing". *Online Journalism Review* [online], March 28. Retrieved: 20. October 2007.
http://www.ojr.org/ojr/kramer/p1017382373.php.

Lasica, J.D. (2002) "Should Newspaper Weblogs Be Subject to the Editing Filter", Online-News discussion list [online], July 1. Retrieved: 26. October 2006
http://talk.poynter.org/online-news/

Lippmann, W. (1922). *Public Opinion*. New York: Macmillan.

Massey, B.L. & Levy, M.R. (1999). "Interactive" Online Journalism at Englishlanguage Web Newspapers in Asia". *Gazette* 61(6), pp. 523-38.

Matheson, D. (2004). "Weblogs and the epistemology of the news: some trends in online journalism". *New Media Society*, 6(1), pp. 443-468.

Maynard, N. (2000). *Mega Media: How Market Forces Are Transforming News*. Victoria, BC: Trafford.

McKinley, M. (2001). "Instant News across Borders: The Computerization of Global Media". In Silvia, T. (ed.) *Global News: Perspectives on the Information Age*. Ames: Iowa State University Press.

Meyer, J. (2007). "Globalization. Theory and Trends". *International Journal of Comparative Sociology*, 48(4), pp. 261-273.

Pavlik, J. (2001) *Journalism and New Media*. New York: Columbia University Press.

Piller, C. (2000). "WebNews Sites Fail toClick". *Los AngelesTimes*, 18 August, A1.

Quinn, G. & Trench, B. (2002). "Online News Media and Their Audiences". *Multimedia Content in the Digital Age (MUDIA) Project* [online]. Retrieved: 20. October 2007. http://www.mudia.org/results/WP1%20Del%201.2%20Web%20version.pdf

Scholte, J. (2006). "Global trade and finance". In Baylis, J. & Smith, S. (eds.), *The Globalization of World Politics*, 3rd edn., Oxford: Oxford University Press, pp. 599-619.

Scott, B. (2005). "A Contemporary History of Digital Journalism". *Television & New Media*, 6(89), pp. 89-126.

Seib, P. (2001). *Going Live: Getting the News Right in a Real-time, Online World.* Lanham, MD: Rowman & Littlefield.

Shepard, A. C. (2000). "Get BIG or Get OUT". *American JournalismReview*, 22(2), pp. 22-29.

Small, J. (2000). "Economics 101 of Internet News". *Nieman Reports,* 54(4), pp. 41-42.

Thurman, N. (2007). "The globalization of journalism online A transatlantic study of news websites and their international readers". *Journalism*, 8(3), pp. 285-307.

Wilson, T. (2004). *The Playfull audience. From talk show viewers to Internet users.* New Jersy: Hampton Press New Mwdia and Policy Series.

Wilson, T. & Tan, H. P. (2005). "Less Tangible Ways of Reading: A ludic way of surfing of online Western news sites". Information, Communication & society, 8(3), pp. 394-416.

YOUR KNOWLEDGE HAS VALUE

- We will publish your bachelor's and
  master's thesis, essays and papers

- Your own eBook and book -
  sold worldwide in all relevant shops

- Earn money with each sale

Upload your text at www.GRIN.com
and publish for free